Scott Foresman Reading

Grade 2

Phonics Workbook

Scott Foresman
Phonics System
™

Scott Foresman

Editorial Offices: Glenview, Illinois • New York, New York
Sales Offices: Reading, Massachusetts • Duluth, Georgia • Glenview, Illinois
Carrollton, Texas • Menlo Park, California

Skill	Page Numbers

The letters *a*, *i*, and *u* stand for short vowel sounds in these words.

cat   pig   bug

Draw a line from each picture to the letter that stands for the short vowel sound in the picture name.

1.

2.

a

3.

4.

i

5.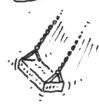

u

6.

7.

a

8.

9.

i

10.

u

Notes for Home: Your child identified words with the short vowel sounds *a*, *i*, and *u*.
Home Activity: Challenge your child to name things with the short *a*, *i*, and *u* vowel sounds and write the words.

Name _____

Read the words with the short *a*, *i*, and *u* vowel sounds.

cat   pig   bug

Circle the word that completes the sentence. Write the word.

1. I like your _____ and coat.   _____

   hut   hat   hit   _____

2. Todd has a small _____ on his hand.   _____

   cat   kit   cut   _____

3. The baby sleeps in a _____.   _____

   crab   crib   cub   _____

4. Kim has a pet _____.   _____

   duck   dig   dark   _____

5. Dan turned on the _____.   _____

   limp   lump   lamp   _____

Notes for Home: Your child wrote words with the short *a, i,* and *u* vowel sounds.
Home Activity: Have your child name words for things he or she can find at the grocery store that have a short *a, i,* or *u* vowel sound.

2

Name _____

A consonant blend can stand for the beginning sound in a word.

broom   **dr**ill   **fl**ute   **tr**ay   **str**eam

Name the pictures in each row. Circle the pictures whose names have the same beginning consonant blend.

1.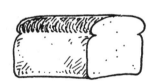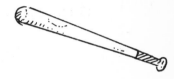

2.

3.

4.

5.

 Notes for Home: Your child identified words with the beginning sounds *br, dr, fl, tr,* and *str.* **Home Activity:** Have your child draw pictures of things that begin with these consonant blends—*br, dr, fl, tr, str.*

3

Name _____

The letter *g* can stand for the sound in *goat* or *gym*.
The letter *c* can stand for the sound in *car* or *cent*.

Circle the pictures that have the same beginning sound.

1.

2.

3.

4.

5.

Notes for Home: Your child reviewed words that begin with the hard and soft *g* and *c* sounds.
Home Activity: Have your child draw pictures of things that can be found in a city and that begin with the hard or soft *g* and the hard or soft *c* sounds.

Double consonants—*ss*, *ll*, and *ff*—can stand for the ending sound in words.

pa**ss**   ca**ll**   o**ff**

Write the letters that stand for the ending sound in the picture name.

1.  _____

2.  _____

3. _____

4.  _____

5. _____

6.  _____

7. _____

8. _____

9.  _____

10. _____

Notes for Home: Your child identified double consonants that stand for the ending sounds in words. **Home Activity:** Help your child write a sentence using two of the words on this page.

The letters *e* and *o* stand for the short vowel sounds in these words.

bed

mop

Circle the word with the same vowel sound as the picture name.

1. pet

cat

2.  top

ten

3. 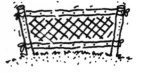 cap

red

4.  sled

sock

5.  bag

pot

6.  hop

pen

7.  cub

dock

8.  nest

plum

9.  mom

map

10.  mask

desk

 Notes for Home: Your child identified words with the short *e* and *o* vowel sounds.
Home Activity: Invite your child to tell a story about a pet using words with the short *e* and *o* vowel sounds.

Name _____

Read the words with the short vowel sounds.

t**e**n   st**o**p

Choose the letter *e* or *o* to finish each word. Write the word.

1. The spider made a w__b.

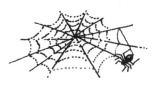

_____
- -
_____

2. The door has a l__ck.

_____
- -
_____

3. The h__n sat on the fence.

_____
- -
_____

4. The t__p spins fast.

_____
- -
_____

5. The ball hit the n__t.

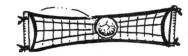

_____
- -
_____

Notes for Home: Your child identified words with the short *e* and *o* vowel sounds.
Home Activity: Read a newspaper or magazine article with your child. Find words with the short *e* or *o* vowel sound.

Name ______________________________

A consonant blend—*ld, nd, nt, mp,* or *st*—can stand for the ending sound in a word.

gold   wind   pint   camp   mist

Circle the letters that stand for the ending sound in the picture name.

1.  la___ mp ld

2.  chi___ ld lt

3.  ne___ ss st

4. 

sta___ nd mp

5.  ba___ nd nk

6.  pai___ nd nt

7.  co___ ld lt

8.  fi___ sk st

9.  po___ nt nd

10.  pla___ ng nt

Notes for Home: Your child identified consonant blends at the end of words.
Home Activity: Write the letters *ld, nd, nt, mp,* and *st* on a sheet of paper and help your child make a list of other words that end in these letters.

© Scott Foresman 2

The *k* sound can be spelled with the letters *c, k,* or *ck*.

ba**c**on   la**k**e   sti**ck**

Circle the letters that stand for /k/. Write the word.

1. du●      c   k   (ck)

                                     duck

2. ●ar      (c)   k   ck

                                     CAr

3. ●ite      c   (k)   ck

                                     kitei

4. ●itten      c   (k)   ck

                                     kitten

5. so ●      c   k   (ck)

                                     sock

 **Notes for Home:** Your child identified letters that stand for the *k* sound.
Home Activity: Have your child draw a picture of things in a park whose names have the *k* sound and then write *c, k,* or *ck* by each picture.

Name _____

These words begin with consonant blends.

broom   **dr**ess   **fl**ute   **str**eet

Use the word part and the consonant blend *br, dr, fl,* or *str* to write a word that finishes the phrase.

I.

     _____ipe

     _____

     a wide _____

2.

     _____ush

     _____

     a big _____

3.

     _____eam

     _____

     a cool _____

4.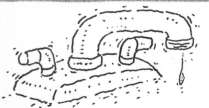

     _____ower

     _____

     a _____ garden

5.

     _____ip

     _____

     a slow _____

Notes for Home: Your child reviewed words that begin with the consonant blends *br, dr, fl,* and *str*. **Home Activity:** Ask your child to write a riddle about one of the words on this page.

10

Name _____

A consonant digraph—*ch*, *th*, *sh*, or *wh*—can stand for the beginning sound in a word.

Circle the word that names the picture. Then write the word.

1.

corn

thorn

_____

2.

please

cheese

_____

3.

shell

well

_____

4.

crumb

thumb

_____

5.

tail

whale

_____

Notes for Home: Your child identified consonant digraphs that stand for beginning sounds in words. **Home Activity:** Have your child make up a tongue twister using words that begin with *ch*, *th*, *sh*, or *wh*.

13

The letters *a, e, i, o,* and *u* are vowels that stand for the short vowel sounds in these words.

cab   red   big   cot   cut

Circle the picture name. Write the word.

1. wig _____

   wag _____

2. shop _____

   ship _____

3. bag _____

   bug _____

4. nut _____

   net _____

5. fin _____

   fan _____

6. dock _____

   desk _____

7. jog _____

   jug _____

8. rod _____

   red _____

9. pin _____

   pan _____

10. bad _____

    bed _____

Notes for Home: Your child reviewed words with short vowel sounds. **Home Activity:** Have your child think of rhyming words for five of the words on this page.

© Scott Foresman 2

Name _____

Each of these words ends with a consonant blend.

li**st**   pai**nt**   ba**nd**   col**d**   ca**mp**

Circle the word to finish the sentence. Write the word.

1. The sun set in the _____.  _____
   west   went

2. Can I _____ the trophy?   _____
   hold   host

3. The pipe was _____. 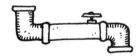 _____
   best   bent

4. The _____ blew hard.  _____
   wild   wind

5. The letter needs a _____.  _____
   stamp   stand

Notes for Home: Your child reviewed words that end with consonant blends *st, nt, nd, mp,* and *ld.* **Home Activity:** Have your child look for a magazine picture whose name ends with a consonant blend and tell a story about the picture.

Name _____

The long *e* sound can be spelled *ea* and *ee*.

t**ea**m   f**ee**d

Circle the picture in each box that has the long *e* sound.

1.

2.

3.

4.

5.

6.

7.

8.

9.
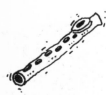 

10.

Notes for Home: Your child identified words with the long *e* sound spelled *ea* and *ee*.
Home Activity: Have your child write a short rhyme using words on this page.

Name _____

The long *e* sound can be spelled *ea* and *ee*.

be**a**ch   thr**ee**

Look at each picture. Choose a word from the box to complete the sentence. Write the word.

---

beans   green   weed   cream   peach

---

1. Who will pick a _____ ?

---

2. Lin pulled up a _____ .

---

3. The ice _____ is melting.

---

4. The grass is _____ .

---

5. The _____ are good to eat.

Notes for Home: Your child identified words with the long *e* sound spelled *ea* and *ee*.
Home Activity: Have your child write a silly newspaper headline using words from this page.

A consonant digraph—*ch, ng, nk, sh,* and *th*—can stand for the ending sound in a word.

Look at the letters. Circle the picture whose name ends with that sound.

1. ch

2. ng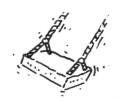

3. nk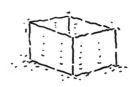

4. sh

5. th

© Scott Foresman 2

 Notes for Home: Your child identified consonant digraphs that stand for ending sounds in words. **Home Activity:** Have your child write sentences using the names for the circled pictures on this page.

Words that end in *e* usually have a long vowel sound.
mate   ride   mule   hose

Circle the word that completes each sentence.

1. I can't find the roll of _____.   tap   tape

2. Ted went down the _____ in the park.   sled   slide

3. The bear slept in the _____.   cab   cave

4. The little cub was _____.   cut   cute

5. There is a _____ in your sweater.   hole   hill

6. An elephant is a _____ animal.   hug   huge

7. Do you _____ to ride your bike?   like   lake

8. The _____ swam in the ocean.   whale   while

9. Put the pan on the _____.   stop   stove

10. You use your _____ to smell things.   not   nose

Notes for Home: Your child reviewed words with long vowel sounds and final *e*.
Home Activity: Have your child look for magazine pictures whose names have long vowel sounds and final *e*, cut them out, and paste them on a sheet of paper.

Name _____

Say each word and listen to the beginning sound.

chair   **th**umb   **sh**oe   **wh**ale

Write the word that goes with each clue.

cheer   thunder   sheep   whisper   chicken

1. a quiet sound only one person can hear

   _____
   - - - - - - - - - - - - - - - - - -
   _____

2. makes a noise that sounds like "b-a-a"

   _____
   - - - - - - - - - - - - - - - - - -
   _____

3. a rumbling sound during a storm

   _____
   - - - - - - - - - - - - - - - - - -
   _____

4. the sound at a game when your team wins

   _____
   - - - - - - - - - - - - - - - - - -
   _____

5. makes a cluck, cluck sound

   _____
   - - - - - - - - - - - - - - - - - -
   _____

Notes for Home: Your child identified consonant digraphs that stand for beginning sounds in words. **Home Activity:** Help your child make a list of words that begin with *ch, th, sh,* and *wh.*

The long *e* sound can be spelled *e* or *y*.

be   busy

Look at each picture. Draw a line from the picture to the word that has the long *e* sound and tells about the picture.

1.

hilly

road

2.

dog

silly

3.

girl

she

4.

bunny

rabbit

5.

sunshine

sunny

Notes for Home: Your child identified words that have the long *e* sound spelled *e* and *y*.
Home Activity: Have your child write a story using words that have the long *e* sound spelled *e* and *y*.

Name _____

> Words like *she* and *silly* have the long *e* sound spelled
> *e* and *y*.

Write the long *e* word to finish the sentence.

me   my

1. Uncle Tim sent _____ a present.

_____

messy   most

2. Nan's room is _____.

_____

very   vase

3. This tree is _____ tall.

_____

be   by

4. Ki will _____ late for school.

_____

funny   first

5. The _____ clown made us laugh.

_____

Notes for Home: Your child identified words that have the long *e* sound spelled *e* and *y*.
Home Activity: Have your child look in magazine or newspaper articles for other words that have the long *e* sound spelled *e* and *y*.

Name _____

The letters *-ed* can be added to the end of some words without changing the spelling of the base word.

paint—paint**ed**   walk—walk**ed**   clean—clean**ed**

Add *-ed* to each word and write the word. Then draw a line to the picture that shows the action.

1. climb _____

   _____

2. play _____

   _____

3. cook _____

   _____

4. yawn _____

   _____

5. laugh _____

   _____

Notes for Home: Your child identified words that do not change spelling when the ending *-ed* is added. **Home Activity:** Have your child write a sentence using each of the words.

Name _____

The letters *ea* and *ee* can spell the long *e* vowel sound.

dr**ea**m   sp**ee**d

Find words in the box to complete the puzzle.

meal	sheep	wreath	teeth
bead	peel	sea	heel

Across
2. circle made of branches
4. skin of an orange
5. body of water

Down
1. lunch or dinner
3. part of your foot

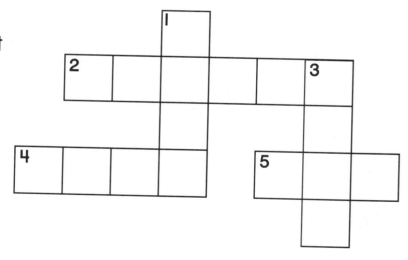

The letters *ch, ng, sh,* and *th* stand for the ending sounds in these words.

lun**ch**   ri**ng**   pu**sh**   boo**th**

Find five words in the puzzle that end with *ch, ng, sh,* or *th.* Circle each word in the puzzle. Then write the word.

m	n	v	u	k
s	w	i	n	g
x	q	k	j	p
o	g	w	l	t
y	b	a	t	h
b	t	s	o	i
z	b	h	y	n
d	e	q	i	g
t	o	u	c	h

1. _____

2. _____

3. _____

4. _____

5. _____

Notes for Home: Your child reviewed consonant digraphs that stand for ending sounds in words. **Home Activity:** Have your child write words that end in *ch, ng, sh,* or *th* and then draw a picture to show the meaning of the words.

Name _____

The letters *a, ai,* and *ay* can spell the long *a* vowel sound.

ta**b**le   **pa**il   st**ay**

Circle the word that names each picture and has the long *a* sound.

1. snow

    snail

2. paint

    pint

3. he

    hay

4. pan

    paper

5. ran

    ray

6. day

    dime

7. track

    train

8. bag

    baby

9. tray

    trap

10. sail

    seal

Notes for Home: Your child identified words that have the long *a* sound spelled *a, ai,* or *ay.*
Home Activity: Encourage your child to choose five words from this page and use each one in a sentence.

Words like *paper, mail,* and *day* have the long *a* sound spelled *a, ai,* and *ay.*

Find a word in the box that rhymes with the underlined word in each sentence. Write the word. Then say the whole rhyme.

| stain | today | table | clay | pail |

_____
----

1. The cat put its <u>tail</u> in a red _____.

_____
----

2. This is the <u>way</u> to mold your _____.

_____
----

3. It's wet and <u>gray</u> outside _____.

_____
----

4. The <u>rain</u> made a big wet _____.

_____
----

5. The <u>cable</u> is behind the _____.

Notes for Home: Your child identified words that have the long *a* sound spelled *a, ai,* or *ay.*
Home Activity: Have your child write *table, rain,* and *way* across the top of a sheet of paper and then find and write words with long *a* sound spelled the same as each word.

Name _____

The letters *-es, -ing,* and *-s* can be added to the end of some words without changing the spelling of the base word.

hatch—hatch**es**   fall—fall**ing**   sit—sit**s**

Add the ending to the new word. Write the new word to finish the phrase.

1. tie   _____ her shoe (**-s**)

2. search   _____ for a lost dog (**-ing**)

3. walk   _____ to school (**-s**)

4. knock   _____ on a door (**-ing**)

5. scratch _____ an itch (**-es**)

Notes for Home: Your child wrote words that do not change spelling when the ending *-es, -ing,* or *-s* is added. **Home Activity:** Have your child think of words that rhyme with the words from this page and then form new words by adding *-es, -ing,* or *-s.*

Name _____

The long *e* sound can be spelled *e* or *y*.

be   hungr**y**

Read the riddles. Write answers that have long *e*.

open	country	little	we	him
tiny	empty	he	farm	us

1. Where do horses and cows live?   _____

2. What size is a mouse?   _____

3. What is a box if it has nothing in it?   _____

4. What is a word for a friend and me?   _____

5. What is a word for a boy?   _____

Notes for Home: Your child wrote words that have the long *e* sound spelled *e* and *y*.
Home Activity: Have your child write each word from this page on a card and then take turns with your child drawing a card and using the word in a sentence.

Words like *jump* and *scold* do not change their spelling when *-ed* is added.

jump—jump**ed**   scold—scold**ed**

Underline the word that will correctly complete the sentence when *-ed* is added. Then write the word with *-ed*.

1. Aunt Erica ____ the car.
   sail   wax

   _____

2. We ____ Dad in the yard.
   help   hop

   _____

3. Troy ____ the picture.
   climb   paint

   _____

4. The dog ____ loudly.
   bark   talk

   _____

5. My sisters ____ the garage.
   jump   clean

   _____

Notes for Home: Your child reviewed words that do not change spelling when the ending *-ed* is added. **Home Activity:** Have your child look through a newspaper article and underline other *-ed* words.

Name _____

The long *i* sound can spelled *i*, *igh*, *y*, or *ie*.

iris   l**igh**t   fr**y**   p**ie**

In each row, circle the picture that goes with the word.
Then say the word.

1. light

2. night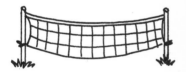

3. fly

4. tie

5. high

 Notes for Home: Your child identified words with the long *i* sound spelled *i*, *igh*, *y*, and *ie*.
Home Activity: Have your child write a short poem about the night using some of these
words: *high, sky, bright, fly, light, delight.*

31

The letters *i*, *igh*, *y*, and *ie* can spell the long *i* sound.

mind   high   cry   tie

Write each word from the box under the word with the same vowel pattern.

right   find   why   pie   idea

List 1
Words like *mind*

1. _____

2. _____

List 2
Words like *high*

3. _____

List 3
Words like *cry*

4. _____

List 4
Words like *tie*

5. _____

Notes for Home: Your child identified words with the long *i* sound spelled *i, igh, y,* and *ie*.
Home Activity: Print words that have the long *i* sound on index cards. Have your child pick a card, say the word, and tell the letter or letters that spell long *i*.

Some words have one consonant in the middle: *cabin*.
Some words have two consonants in the middle: *kitten*.

Say each word. Write the number **1** or **2** to tell how many consonants are in the middle of the word. Then write the words that have two middle consonants.

1. wagon _____
2. follow _____
3. bottom _____
4. tunnel _____
5. metal _____
6. dresser _____
7. pillow _____
8. water _____
9. butter _____
10. lizard _____
11. hippo _____
12. puppy _____
13. tiger _____
14. river _____
15. yogurt _____

_____ _____

_____ _____

_____ _____

_____ _____

_____ _____

_____ _____

_____ _____

Notes for Home: Your child identified words with one and two consonants in the middle. **Home Activity:** Have your child write a sentence using each of the animal words from the page.

The letter *a* can stand for the long *a* sound: *paper*.
The letters *ai* can stand for the long *a* sound: *mail*.
The letters *ay* can stand for the long *a* sound: *day*.

Read the clue by each picture. Draw a line to the word that tells about the picture and has the long *a* sound.

1. follows an animal

nail

home

2. a place to eat

spray

saw

3. month for flowers

water

tail

4. goes with a hammer

table

June

5. makes things wet

wagon

May

Notes for Home: Your child identified words that have the long *a* sound spelled *a*, *ai*, or *ay*.
Home Activity: Have your child write sentences about a spring day using words like *May*, *jay*, *snail*, *bait*, and *day*.

Name _____

Words like *reach*, *bark*, and *sleep* do not change their spelling when *-es*, *-ing*, or *-s* is added.

reach—reach**es**   bark—bark**ing**   sleep—sleep**s**

Unscramble each word and write the correct word.

1. Pedro _____ a letter to a friend.
   estwri

2. Liz looks both ways before she _____ the street.
   ssesorc

3. Sam _____ out the candle.
   swobl

4. The barber _____ Pete's hair.
   tucs

5. Jana is _____ in the parade.
   gnrachim

Notes for Home: Your child identified words that do not change spelling when the ending *-es*, *-ing*, or *-s* is added. **Home Activity:** Have your child add *-es*, *-ing*, and *-s* to the words *push*, *color*, and *talk* to make new words and then write a sentence using each word.

© Scott Foresman 2

The letters *er, ir,* and *ur* stand for the vowel sound in these words.

h**er**   f**ir**st   t**ur**n

Say each picture name. Circle the word that names the picture. Write the word and circle the letters that stand for the vowel-*r* sound.

1.    hut   huge   turtle   _____

2.    dirt   skirt   set   _____

3.    desk   germ   clerk   _____

4.    burn   purse   prune   _____

5.    first   stir   five   _____

 Notes for Home: Your child identified the letters that stand for an *r*-controlled vowel sound. **Home Activity:** Have your child write a story about one of the pictures.

Name _____

The vowel sound in *perch*, *skirt*, and *nurse* is spelled *er, ir,* and *ur*.

Find words in the box to complete the puzzle.

perk	dirt	serve	perch
thirsty	burn	purse	fir

Across
2. needing a drink of water
5. small bag

Down
1. evergreen tree
3. offer food to
4. bird's resting place

Notes for Home: Your child used words with *r*-controlled vowels to complete a crossword puzzle. **Home Activity:** Have your child cut out magazine pictures whose names contain *r*-controlled vowels *(germs, clerk, herd, dirt, fir, shirt, skirt, bird, burn, fur)*.

Name _____

To form the plural of many words, add *-s*. To form the plural of words that end in *ch, sh, s, ss,* or *x,* add *-es*. To form the plural of words that end in a consonant and *y,* change the *y* to *i* before adding *-es*.

Each picture shows two or more of something. Read the word and write the plural form of the word.

1. letter

_____

2. pony

_____

3. glass

_____

4. fox

_____

5. puppy

_____

Notes for Home: Your child formed the plural of words by adding *-s* or *-es* to the base word.
Home Activity: Have your child look through advertisements and list plural words. Encourage your child to underline the letters that are used to form each plural.

Words like *tiger*, *sign*, *try*, and *lie* have the long *i* sound spelled *i, igh, y,* and *ie*.

Name the picture. Write the word with the long *i* sound to complete the phrase.

tie   pit

1. _____

a black _____

warm   bright

2. the _____ sunshine

dark   high

3. a _____ cloud

wild   wet

4. a _____ animal

shy   funny

5. a _____ student

Notes for Home: Your child identified words with the long *i* sound spelled *i, igh, y,* and *ie*.
Home Activity: Have your child make a list of words in which the long *i* vowel sound is spelled *i, igh, y,* or *ie*.

Name _____

Yogurt and *spider* have one consonant in the middle.
Paddle and *rattle* have double consonants in the middle.

Circle the word that completes the sentence. Write each circled word in the correct list.

1. The ___ slept near the fireplace.   kennel   kitten

2. The dog liked to ride in the ___.   wagon   waffle

3. Drop the ___ in the mailbox.   lever   letter

4. The clown made the girl ___.   gobble   giggle

5. Our ___ is near a lake.   cabin   copper

Double consonants

- - - - - - - - - - - - - - - - -
_____
_____
- - - - - - - - - - - - - - - - -
_____
_____
- - - - - - - - - - - - - - - - -
_____

Single consonants

- - - - - - - - - - - - - - - - -
_____
_____
- - - - - - - - - - - - - - - - -
_____

Notes for Home: Your child identified words with one or two consonants in the middle.
Home Activity: Help your child think of other words with one or two middle consonants and list them on a sheet of paper.

Name _____

The long *o* sound can be spelled with the letters *o, oa, ow,* or *oe*.

only   fl**oa**t   gr**ow**   h**oe**

Look at each picture. Write the long *o* word for the picture.

1.  _____

2.  _____

3.  _____

4. _____

5.  _____

6. _____

7. _____

8. _____

9.  _____

10. _____

Notes for Home: Your child identified words with the long *o* sound spelled *o, oa, ow,* or *oe*.
Home Activity: Have your child write a sentence using four words from this page and draw a picture to go with the sentence.

The long *o* sound can be spelled with the letters *o, oa, ow,* or *oe*.

go   toad   slow   toe

Write the words that have the long *o* sound inside the giant *o*.

road	low	blow	load
hop	foam	box	clock
goal	top	no	lock
told	fox	only	hoe

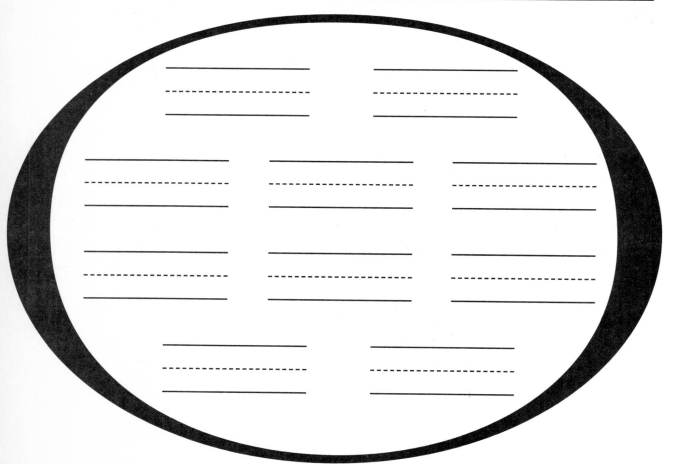

Notes for Home: Your child identified words with the long *o* sound spelled *o, oa, ow,* or *oe*.
Home Activity: Have your child write sentences about a boat trip using the words *boat, float, slow, old,* and *row*.

Name _____

A compound word is a word made up of two smaller words.

air + plane = airplane   birth + day = birthday

Circle each compound word. Write the compound words.

1. teacher
2. baseball
3. animal

4. afternoon
5. pencil
6. anyone

7. sentence
8. sidewalk
9. outside

10. person
11. doorbell
12. question

13. doghouse
14. notebook
15. tiger

_____   _____   _____
- - - - - - - - - - -   - - - - - - - - - - -   - - - - - - - - - - -
_____   _____   _____

_____   _____   _____
- - - - - - - - - - -   - - - - - - - - - - -   - - - - - - - - - - -
_____   _____   _____

_____   _____
- - - - - - - - - - -   - - - - - - - - - - -
_____   _____

Notes for Home: Your child identified compound words. **Home Activity:** Write the words *down, town, rain, drop, sun, shine, bed, room, every, thing, my,* and *self* on cards and have your child put the cards together to make compound words.

Name _____

The letters *er, ir,* and *ur* stand for the same vowel sound.

p**er**k　　　g**ir**l　　　h**ur**t

Write a word from the box to complete each tongue twister.
Then underline the letters that stand for the vowel sound.

perch	dirt	fir	turn	serve

1. Sandy will _____ salad in a seashell.

2. Please put Polly Parrot on her _____.

3. Dale's dog Dixie dug deep in the _____.

4. It's Tina's _____ to take a trip.

5. The forest was full of fat _____ trees.

Notes for Home: Your child wrote words with *r*-controlled vowels. **Home Activity:** Help your child look through a book and find words that have the same vowel sound as *girl*.

44

© Scott Foresman 2

Name _____

The endings -s and -es are added to words to form the plural. For words that end in a consonant and y, the y is changed to i before -es is added.

jet—jet**s**	box—box**es**	bench—bench**es**
wish—wish**es**	circus—circus**es**	baby—bab**ies**

Write the word that fits each clue. Then write the plural form of the word.

ocean   penny   lunch   cherry   bunny

1. rabbit   _____   _____

2. meal   _____   _____

3. red fruit   _____   _____

4. one cent   _____   _____

5. a whale's home   _____   _____

Notes for Home: Your child formed the plurals of words by adding -s or -es. **Home Activity:** Have your child write the words *hand, ax, beach, crash,* and *story* and then write the plural of each word by adding -s or -es.

45

Name _____

The letters *ce* and *se* spell the sound at the end of *place* and *house*. The letters *se* can also spell the sound at the end of *please*. The letters *ge* spell the sound at the end of *huge*.

Write a word from the box that makes sense in each phrase.

page	dance	these	face	mouse

1. wash your _____

2. _____ shoes

3. a field _____

4. read _____ 354

5. a tap _____

Notes for Home: Your child wrote words that end with the *s, z,* and *j* sounds spelled *ce, se,* and *ge*. **Home Activity:** Have your child make up one sentence using two words that end in *ce* or *se* and another sentence using two words that end in *ge*.

46

© Scott Foresman 2

Name _____

The letters *ce* spell the sound at the end of *place*. The letters *se* spell the sounds at the end of *base* and *please*. The letters *ge* spell the sound at the end of *huge*.

Use the letters *ce*, *ge*, or *se* to finish the word. Then write the word.

 1. pa___
_____
- - - - - - - - - - - - - - -
_____

 2. ro___
_____
- - - - - - - - - - - - - - -
_____

 3. hou___
_____
- - - - - - - - - - - - - - -
_____

 4. fen___
_____
- - - - - - - - - - - - - - -
_____

 5. ca___
_____
- - - - - - - - - - - - - - -
_____

 6. no___
_____
- - - - - - - - - - - - - - -
_____

 7. ra___
_____
- - - - - - - - - - - - - - -
_____

 8. ri___
_____
- - - - - - - - - - - - - - -
_____

 9. ho___
_____
- - - - - - - - - - - - - - -
_____

 10. mou___
_____
- - - - - - - - - - - - - - -
_____

 Notes for Home: Your child wrote words that end with the *s, z,* and *j* sounds spelled *ce, se,* and *ge*. **Home Activity:** Have your child write a two-line poem using rhyming words such as *cage—page, nose—rose, rice—nice,* or *house—mouse.*

Name _____

A word that shows ownership ends with an *'s* or *s'*.

teacher—teacher**'s**

teachers—teacher**s'**

Circle the words that describe the picture.

1.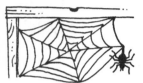

   the spider's web

   the spiders web

2.

   the babies mother

   the babies' mother

3.

   the planes wings

   the plane's wings

4.

   the elephant's trunk

   the elephants' trunks

5.

   the childrens school

   the children's school

Notes for Home: Your child identified words that show ownership. **Home Activity:** Have your child make a list of things in the house and then write words that tell who the things belong to.

48

© Scott Foresman 2

Name _____

The letters *o, oa, ow,* and *oe* stand for the long *o* vowel sound.

so   b**oa**t   **ow**n   h**oe**

Write a word from the list to complete each phrase. Then circle the letters that stand for the long *o* sound.

grow	goat	show	goal	float
only	throw	blow	toe	cold

1. _____ a ball

2. scored a _____

3. an _____ child

4. stubbed her _____

5. a _____ winter day

Notes for Home: Your child identified words with the long *o* sound spelled *o, oa, ow,* or *oe.*
Home Activity: Have your child choose a word from the page and think of a word that rhymes with it.

Two smaller words put together make a compound word.

side + walk = sidewalk   any + thing = anything

Write the two words that make up each compound word.

I. raincoat = _____ + _____

2. doghouse = _____ + _____

3. mailbox = _____ + _____

4. cookbook = _____ + _____

5. bedroom = _____ + _____

Notes for Home: Your child identified words that make up compound words.
Home Activity: Have your child use each compound word in a sentence.

The letters *ou* stand for the vowel sound in *out*.
The letters *ow* stand for the vowel sound in *down*.

Circle the word in each row that has the same vowel sound as *out* and *down*.

I.	rope	clock	cow
2.	mouse	pop	soap
3.	frown	cot	rose
4.	hole	cob	found
5.	block	crown	smoke
6.	pound	born	hose
7.	bounce	note	hot
8.	float	ground	mop
9.	dog	lock	south
10.	brown	mom	nose

Notes for Home: Your child identified words with the vowel sound in *out*.
Home Activity: Have your child write four sentences using *ou* and *ow* words from this page.

The letters *ou* and *ow* stand for the vowel sound in *count* and *cow.*

Choose the letters *ou* or *ow* to finish each word. Write the word.

1. We watched the
   funny cl_____n.

_____

2. The s_____nd of
   thunder woke me up.

_____

3. The baby kangaroo hid
   in the p_____ch.

_____

4. The unhappy boy had
   a fr_____n on his face.

_____

5. Use a t_____el to dry
   the dishes.

_____

Notes for Home: Your child wrote *ou* and *ow* words. **Home Activity:** Have your child use *ou* and *ow* words to tell a story about a mouse going to town.

52

Name _____

When a word ends with one vowel followed by one consonant, the final consonant is doubled before *-ed* or *-ing* is added.

drip—dripp**ed**   hug—hugg**ing**

Follow the signs to make a new word. Write the word.

1. trip + ed
_____
- - - - - - - - - - - - - - - - - - -
_____

2. swim + ing
_____
- - - - - - - - - - - - - - - - - - - -
_____

3. stop + ing
_____
- - - - - - - - - - - - - - - - - - -
_____

4. run + ing
_____
- - - - - - - - - - - - - - - - - - - -
_____

5. pat + ed
_____
- - - - - - - - - - - - - - - - - - -
_____

6. mop + ed
_____
- - - - - - - - - - - - - - - - - - - -
_____

7. let + ing
_____
- - - - - - - - - - - - - - - - - - -
_____

8. shrug + ed
_____
- - - - - - - - - - - - - - - - - - - -
_____

9. hop + ed
_____
- - - - - - - - - - - - - - - - - - -
_____

10. bat + ing
_____
- - - - - - - - - - - - - - - - - - - -
_____

© Scott Foresman 2

Notes for Home: Your child doubled the final consonant in words before adding *-ed* and *-ing*.
Home Activity: Have your child write five sentences using words from this page.

The letters *ce* and *se* spell the sound at the end of *race* and *mouse*. The letters *se* can also spell the sound at the end of *tease*. The letters *ge* spell the sound at the end of *cage*.

Find five words in the puzzle that end with *ce, ge,* or *se*. Circle each word in the puzzle. Then write the word.

p	e	f	c	e
l	p	a	g	e
e	t	c	d	h
a	h	e	i	o
s	e	b	s	u
e	g	e	e	s
j	u	i	c	e

1. _____

2. _____

3. _____

4. _____

5. _____

Notes for Home: Your child wrote words that end with the *s, z,* and *j* sounds spelled *ce, se,* and *ge*. **Home Activity:** Have your child write two words that end in *ce, se,* or *ge* and then draw a picture to go with each word.

Name _____

A possessive word ends with 's or s'.

Betty**'s** book   the girl**s'** shoes

Add 's or s' to the underlined word to show ownership.

1. the desks of the <u>students</u>

   _____

   the --------------------------- desks

2. the book of <u>Miguel</u>

   _____

   --------------------------- book

3. the buttons of the <u>shirt</u>

   _____

   the --------------------------- buttons

4. the playground of the <u>school</u>

   _____

   the --------------------------- playground

5. the uniforms of the <u>players</u>

   _____

   the --------------------------- uniforms

 Notes for Home: Your child added 's or s' to words to show ownership.
Home Activity: Write the names of familiar people and objects on one side of cards and have your child write the possessive forms of the words on the other side.

© Scott Foresman 2

55

Name _____

> The letters *ar* stand for the vowel sound in *card*.

Circle the word that completes each sentence and has the same vowel sound as *card*. Write the word.

1. The kitten plays with _____.

   yarn   me

   _____

2. Uncle Lin bought a new _____.

   bike   car

   _____

3. We saw a _____ in the ocean.

   shark   whale

   _____

4. The band will _____ .

   play   march

   _____

5. Put the marbles in a _____.

   jar   sack

   _____

56

Name _____

The letters *ar* stand for the vowel sound in *car*.

Write the *ar* word that means the opposite of each word.

| part | hard | start | far | dark |

1. finish   _____

2. near   _____

3. light   _____

4. whole   _____

5. soft   _____

Notes for Home: Your child wrote *ar* words. **Home Activity:** Have your child look for magazine pictures of objects whose names have the same vowel sound as *car*.

Name _____

When a word ends with *e*, the *e* is dropped before *-ed* or *-ing* is added.

smile—smil**ed**   ride—rid**ing**

Choose the word that makes sense in the sentence. Add the ending and write the word.

1. My cousin is _____ _____ to Ohio. (**-ing**)

    move   judge

2. I _____ _____ the book I read. (**-ed**)

    like   time

3. Uncle Rio _____ _____ a loaf of bread. (**-ed**)

    bake   rake

4. The runners _____ _____ around the track. (**-ed**)

    trace   race

5. Claire is _____ _____ a letter to her pen pal. (**-ing**)

    care   write

Notes for Home: Your child dropped the final *e* in words before adding *-ed* and *-ing*.
Home Activity: Take turns with your child choosing a word from the page and telling what it means.

Name _____

The letters *ou* and *ow* stand for the vowel sound in the words *count* and *cow*.

Write the word that goes with the other words in each group and has the vowel sound in *cow*.

south	brown	north	flower	sponge
farm	towel	owl	juggler	sofa
hawk	rat	blue	couch	town
mouse	grass	crown	queen	clown

1. bath, soap, _____

_____

2. tree, plant, _____

_____

3. east, west, _____

_____

4. squirrel, rabbit, _____

_____

5. eagle, robin, _____

_____

6. castle, king, _____

_____

7. chair, stool, _____

_____

8. acrobat, ringmaster, _____

_____

9. city, village, _____

_____

10. red, green, _____

_____

Notes for Home: Your child identified *ou* and *ow* words. **Home Activity:** Have your child find two words on this page that rhyme and write a riddle using them.

Name ____________________

Some words double the final consonant when *-ed* and *-ing* are added.

clap—clap**ped**—clap**ping**

Each number stands for a letter of the alphabet. Use the code to write each word. Then add *-ed* and *-ing* to the word.

1	2	3	4	5	6	7	8	9	10	11	12	13
a	b	d	h	g	i	l	m	p	r	s	t	u

	Code word	with *-ed*	with *-ing*
1.	3 + 6 + 9		
2.	4 + 13 + 5		
3.	11 + 7 + 1 + 8		
4.	5 + 10 + 1 + 2		
5.	12 + 10 + 6 + 9		

Notes for Home: Your child doubled the final consonant in words before adding *-ed* and *-ing*. **Home Activity:** Have your child add *-ed* and *-ing* to *tap, sip,* and *tip*.

Name _____

The letters *ew*, *oo*, and *ou* can spell the same vowel sound.

dr**ew**   r**oo**m   y**ou**

Circle the word that names each picture. Then write the circled word in the correct column.

1.    soup

loop

2.    zoom

moon

3.    knew

grew

4.    broom

boom

5.    blew

crew

Vowel sound spelled *ew*

_____
- - - - - - - - - - - - - -
_____

_____
- - - - - - - - - - - - - -
_____

Vowel sound spelled *oo*

_____
- - - - - - - - - - - - - -
_____

_____
- - - - - - - - - - - - - -
_____

Vowel sound spelled *ou*

_____
- - - - - - - - - - - - - -
_____

Notes for Home: Your child identified words with the vowel patterns *ew*, *oo*, and *ou*.
Home Activity: Read the circled words together and make up sentences for the words.

Name _____

The letters *ew*, *oo*, and *ou* can spell the same vowel sound.

bl**ew**　　　l**oo**p　　　gr**ou**p

Follow the directions in each sentence. Use words from the list.

drew　　　cool　　　goose　　　grew　　　soup

1. Write the word that rhymes with *pool*. Circle the way the vowel sound is spelled.

2. Write the word that rhymes with *new*. Circle the way the vowel sound is spelled.

3. Write the word for a large bird. Circle the way the vowel sound is spelled.

4. Write the word that rhymes with *group*. Circle the way the vowel sound is spelled.

5. Write the word for what an artist did. Circle the way the vowel sound is spelled.

Notes for Home: Your child identified words with the vowel patterns *ew*, *oo*, and *ou*. **Home Activity:** Have your child make up a story using the words *flew, cool, ooze, grew,* and *balloon*.

Name _____

A contraction is a shorter way of writing two words.
An apostrophe takes the place of the letter or letters
that are left out.

Circle the words that are used to make the contraction.

1. wasn't	was not were not would not	**2.** you'll	you are you will you were
3. they're	they will they would they are	**4.** he's	he was he is he will
5. we've	we were we will we have	**6.** didn't	do not did not has not

Use one of the contractions above to complete each sentence.

7. Eric says _____ going home.

8. Nita _____ at school today.

9. I know _____ like the movie.

10. We _____ see Shawna there.

Notes for Home: Your child identified words used in contractions. **Home Activity:** Have your child look through a magazine or newspaper article and underline contractions.

The letters *ar* stand for the vowel sound in these words.

p**ar**t   b**ar**n   m**ar**ch

Use the words in the box to complete the puzzle.

| star | carve | yard | scarf | smart |

Across
1. clever
3. cut into slices
4. Let's play in the ___.

Down
1. shines in the sky
2. You wear it around your neck.

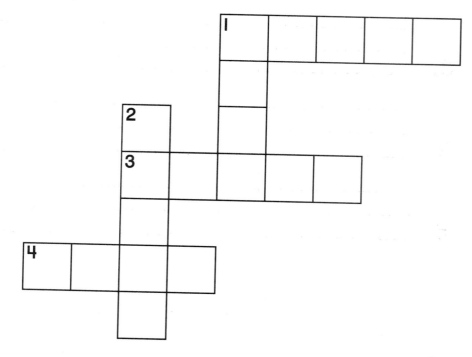

Notes for Home: Your child used words with the *ar* vowel sound to complete the puzzle.
Home Activity: Work with your child to list other words with the *ar* vowel sound.

64

Name _____

When a word ends in *e*, the *e* is dropped before *-ed* or *-ing* is added.

car**e**—car**ed**   hik**e**—hik**ing**

Write each word. Then write the word with *-ed* and *-ing*.

| rake | smile | trace | like | skate |

Word	**Add -ed**	**Add -ing**
1.		
2.		
3.		
4.		
5.		

Notes for Home: Your child dropped the final *e* in words before adding *-ed* and *-ing*.
Home Activity: Look through a newspaper together to find words that follow this pattern. Make a list of the words.

Name _____

Read the words and listen for the vowel sound.

| h**or**n | m**ore** | fl**oor** | f**our** |

Write the *r*-controlled vowel word used in each sentence.

1. She will pour the water.

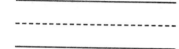

2. It is cooler on the porch.

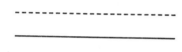

3. Joel knocked on the front door.

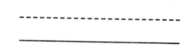

4. The score of the game was 6 to 3.

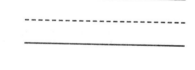

5. The horse ran through the meadow.

Notes for Home: Your child identified words with the *or, ore, oor,* and *our* vowel patterns.
Home Activity: Write the letters *or, ore, oor,* and *our* on paper and help your child write other words with these vowel patterns.

Name _____

The letters *or, ore, oor,* and *our* stand for the vowel sound in these words.

co**r**n   **t**ore   **d**oor   **f**our

Write the word that answers the question. Draw a line under the letters that stand for the vowel sound.

1. Do you blow a cork or a horn?

2. Is ten more or less than six?

3. Do you sit on the door or the floor?

4. Is a storm or a stork a bird?

5. Do you core or pour a glass of milk?

Notes for Home: Your child wrote words with the *or, ore, oor,* and *our* vowel patterns.
Home Activity: Help your child write questions using these vowel-*r* words: *porch, before, court.*

Name _____

If the base word ends in *y*, the *y* is changed to *i* before *-ed* or *-es* is added.

If the base word ends in *y*, the *y* stays when *-ing* is added.

carry—carr**ies**—carr**ied**—carr**ying**

Write each word from the box under the heading that tells what happens to the base word when *-ed, -es,* or *-ing* is added.

hurries	crying	dried	worrying	tries
fried	trying	prying	drying	supplied

No change

1. _____

2. _____

3. _____

4. _____

5. _____

Change *y* to *i*

6. _____

7. _____

8. _____

9. _____

10. _____

Notes for Home: Your child identified words in which the spelling changes before *-ed* or *-es* is added. **Home Activity:** Have your child write the base words for the words on this page.

Name _____

The letters *ew, oo,* and *ou* can spell the same vowel sound.

n**ew**   z**oo**m   gr**ou**p

Write the word that matches each clue. Draw a line under the letters that stand for the vowel sound in the word.

you	soup	stool	drew	spoons

1. food made by boiling
   vegetables or meat

   _____

2. eating tools

   _____

3. something to sit on

   _____

4. made a picture

   _____

5. the person spoken to

   _____

Notes for Home: Your child wrote words with the vowel patterns *ew, oo,* and *ou.*
Home Activity: Help your child write a rhyming word for each word on this page.

An apostrophe (') takes the place of the letter or letters that are left out when two smaller words are written as a contraction.

do not—don't

Write the contraction for the underlined words in each sentence.

_____
----
1. Leah says <u>she is</u> going home. _____

_____
----
2. <u>You are</u> late for dinner. _____

_____
----
3. <u>We have</u> been playing basketball. _____

_____
----
4. Iyo <u>did not</u> water the plants. _____

_____
----
5. <u>I will</u> meet you at the library. _____

The letters *oo* and *ou* stand for the same vowel sound in these words.

look   **cou**ld

Circle each word that has the same vowel sound as the picture name.

cook

woods   soup

should   hood   shook

took   goat   would   count

stood   too   good   though

brook   couldn't   found

moon   bounce

© Scott Foresman 2

Notes for Home: Your child identified words with the vowel patterns *oo* and *ou*.
Home Activity: Help your child write a paragraph using the words *cook, shook, took,* and *book.*

The letters *oo* and *ou* stand for the vowel sound in these words.

to**o**k   c**ou**ld

Write the word that has the same vowel sound as the first word in the row.

hood   1. school   book   room   _____

should   2. around   couldn't   dough   _____

cook   3. woods   zoom   tooth   _____

good   4. wouldn't   you   tool   _____

foot   5. flour   brook   pool   _____

Notes for Home: Your child identified words with the vowel patterns *oo* and *ou*.
Home Activity: Have your child write a book title using one word with the *oo* vowel pattern and one word with the *ou* vowel pattern.

Name _____

The *y* is changed to *i* before *-es* and *-ed* is added if the base word ends in *y*.

The *y* is kept when *-ing* is added if the base word ends in *y*.

dr**y**   dr**ies**   dr**ied**   dry**ing**

Add *-ed* to each word. Write the word.

1. try _____

2. pry _____

3. marry _____

4. reply _____

Add *-es* to each word. Write the word.

5. fry _____

6. cry _____

7. carry _____

8. worry _____

Add *-ing* to each word. Write the word.

9. fly _____

10. hurry _____

Notes for Home: Your child changed the spelling of base words before adding *-ed* or *-es*. **Home Activity:** Have your child choose four words from this page and write a sentence using each one.

The letters *ear* and *eer* stand for the vowel sound in these words.

n**ear**   d**eer**

Underline the words in the box that have the same vowel sound as *near* and *deer*. Then write each underlined word next to its meaning.

clear	read	break	year	beard
cheer	leather	head	steer	great

1. twelve months   _____

2. grows on the chin   _____

3. an animal   _____

4. shout or yell   _____

5. can see through   _____

Notes for Home: Your child identified words with the *r*-controlled vowels *ear* and *eer*.
Home Activity: Work together with your child and make up sentences using the words he or she wrote.

The letters *ear* and *eer* stand for the vowel sound in these words.

dear   **st**e**er**

Choose a word to finish the sentence that has the vowel sound in *dear* and *steer*. Write the word. Then circle the letters that spell the vowel sound.

1. We used _____ tape to seal it.

clear   sticky

2. The shed is _____ the trees.

by   near

3. The crowd _____ for the team.

cheers   yells

4. I didn't _____ the bell ring.

make   hear

5. A _____ ran across the road.

deer   doe

Notes for Home: Your child identified words with the *r*-controlled vowels *ear* and *eer*.
Home Activity: Help your child make a list of other words with this vowel sound.

When the suffix *-ly* is added to a base word, it makes a new word that tells how something is done. If the base word ends in *y,* the *y* is changed to *i* before *-ly* is added.

swift—swift**ly**   happy—happ**ily**

Add *-ly* to the base word to make a new word. Then use each new word to complete a sentence. Some words may work in more than one sentence.

1. bright _____   2. quiet _____

3. slow _____   4. loud _____

5. busy _____

6. Speak _____ when you are in a library.

7. The snail _____ crawled through the garden.

8. The airplane roared _____ overhead.

9. We were _____ decorating the room.

10. The candle shines _____.

Notes for Home: Your child added the suffix *-ly* to base words.
Home Activity: Challenge your child to think of words that describe the following actions: *dressed, stirred, slept, sang, played.*

Name _____

The letters *oo* and *ou* stand for the vowel sound in these words.

h**oo**d   w**ou**ld

Choose a word to complete each sentence. Circle the letters that spell the vowel sound.

1. We sailed little boats in the _____ .
   brook   book

2. I think that is a _____ idea.
   good   wood

3. _____ you help me with my homework?
   Cook   Could

4. I _____ hands with the mayor.
   should   shook

5. Sam _____ the bus to school.
   look   took

Notes for Home: Your child wrote words with the vowel patterns *oo* and *ou*.
Home Activity: Have your child identify rhyming words from this page.

Name _____

The endings *-er* and *-est* are added to a base word to compare things.

smaller** than a ladybug   the littl**est** flower in the garden

---

Choose the best word to complete the sentence. Add *-er* or *-est* and write the new word.

1. This line is _____ than that one.
   long   clean

2. The white kitten is the _____ one of all.
   cute   dark

3. A turtle is _____ than a rabbit.
   slow   fast

4. My pillow is _____ than yours.
   wet   soft

5. A pencil is _____ than a book.
   fat   thin

Notes for Home: Your child used words with *-er* and *-est* endings to make comparisons.
Home Activity: Have your child cut out a magazine picture and write a sentence about the picture using *-er* or *-est* to make a comparison.

© Scott Foresman 2

Name _____

The letters *oi* and *oy* stand for the vowel sound in these words.

bo**i**l   **j**oy

Circle each word that has the same vowel sound as the picture name.

1.

join	phone	pint	dime
choose	toy	chin	road
tiny	point	try	rid
joy	dirt	voice	royal

Write one of the circled words to complete each phrase. You will not use all the words. _____

2. the pencil's sharp _____

3. a loud _____

4. the baby's favorite _____

5. _____ the team

Notes for Home: Your child wrote words with the vowel diphthongs *oi* and *oy*.
Home Activity: Work with your child to make up meaning clues for *noise, foil, loyal,* and *destroy.*

Name _____

The letters *oi* and *oy* stand for the vowel sound in *join* and *royal*.

Circle the *oi* or *oy* word that completes each sentence. Write the word.

1. Sam put the ____ in his bank.

   coin _____

   oil _____

2. Did you hear a loud ____?

   choice _____

   noise _____

3. The ____ ran in the race.

   toy _____

   boy _____

4. Do you ____ playing ball?

   annoy _____

   enjoy _____

5. Our garden has rich ____.

   soil _____

   joint _____

Notes for Home: Your child wrote words with the vowel diphthongs *oi* and *oy*.
Home Activity: Have your child read the five words that were *not* circled on the page and make up a sentence using each one.

Name _____

The suffix *-ful* can be added to a base word.

forget + ful = forget**ful**

Add *-ful* to each base word. Write the new word.

1. color _____

2. care _____

3. harm _____

4. power _____

5. peace _____

6. grace _____

7. play _____

8. hope _____

9. help _____

10. cheer _____

Notes for Home: Your child added the suffix *-ful* to base words. **Home Activity:** Take turns with your child choosing a *-ful* word from the page and making up a silly sentence using the word.

Name _____

The letters *ear* and *eer* stand for the vowel sound in *fear* and *deer*.

Use the code to write each word. Then read the letter.

1	2	3	4	5	6	7	8	9
a	d	e	g	h	n	r	s	y

Dear Rusty,

Sam and I go camping every (1.) _____.

$9 + 3 + 1 + 7$

We put our (2.) _____ in the car.

$4 + 3 + 1 + 7$

We drive to a camp (3.) _____ a stream.

$6 + 3 + 1 + 7$

We hike along (4.) _____ rock cliffs.

$8 + 5 + 3 + 3 + 7$

We see (5.) _____ as we hike.

$2 + 3 + 3 + 7$

Your friend,

Mari

Notes for Home: Your child wrote words with the *r*-controlled vowels *ear* and *eer*.
Home Activity: Help your child use the words on the page to write two-line rhymes.

© Scott Foresman 2

The suffix *-ly* can be added to a base word to make a new word.

quick—quick**ly**   pretty—prett**ily**

Choose a word from the box to answer each clue. Add *-ly* to the base word and write the word. Some words can answer more than one clue.

swift	quiet	sad	happy	slow

1. how the children played in the park   _____

2. how a fox runs   _____

3. how the boy spoke in the library   _____

4. how the girl looked at her broken doll   _____

5. how a turtle moves   _____

Notes for Home: Your child added the suffix *-ly* to base words. **Home Activity:** Have your child choose three *-ly* words from the page and write a sentence for each word.

Name _____

The word *ready* has the short *e* sound spelled with the letters *ea*.

Say the two picture names. Write the word that has the short *e* vowel sound spelled *ea* as in *ready*.

1.  _____

2.   _____

3.   _____

4.  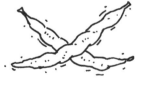 _____

5.   _____

 **Notes for Home:** Your child identified words with the short *e* vowel sound spelled *ea*.
Home Activity: Together make up a sentence for each picture name with the short *e* vowel sound.

The short *e* sound can be spelled *ea*.

Underline the words with the same vowel sound as *ready*. Then follow the directions.

treasure	great	dead	steak	wealth
breakfast	weather	break	bread	head
real	sweater	leave	heavy	meadow

I. Write the word that names a meal.

_____

2. Write the word that rhymes with *feather*.

_____

3. Write the word that means a great deal of money.

_____

4. Write the word that names something to eat.

_____

5. Write the word that names part of the body.

_____

© Scott Foresman 2

Notes for Home: Your child identified words with the short *e* vowel sound spelled *ea*.
Home Activity: Look through a newspaper together to find words with short *e* spelled *ea*.

Name _____

When you add the suffix *-er* to a word, you make a new word that means a person or thing that does something.

bake—bak**er**   jog—jog**ger**

Add *-er* to the word that tells about the picture. Write the new word.

1.

play
paint

_____

- - - - - - - - - - - - - - -

_____

2.

help
farm

_____

- - - - - - - - - - - - - - -

_____

3.

work
dance

_____

- - - - - - - - - - - - - - -

_____

4.

skate
run

_____

- - - - - - - - - - - - - - -

_____

5.

mix
clean

_____

- - - - - - - - - - - - - - -

_____

Notes for Home: Your child added the suffix *-er* to make new words.
Home Activity: Together add *-er* to the other words on the page.

Name _____

The letters *oi* and *oy* stand for the vowel sound in the words *foil* and *toy*.

Choose a word from the box that can replace the underlined word or words in each sentence. Write the word.

moist	boil	boy	joy	soil

1. We planted seeds in the <u>dirt</u>.

_____
_____

2. Saad washed his face with a <u>wet</u> cloth.

_____
_____

3. The <u>young man</u> rode his bike to school.

_____
_____

4. The water in the pot began to <u>cook rapidly</u>.

_____
_____

5. Her heart was filled with <u>happiness</u>.

_____
_____

Notes for Home: Your child wrote words with the vowel diphthongs *oi* and *oy*.
Home Activity: Have your child choose two words from the page and write a riddle about each word.

89

Name _____

The suffix *-ful* can be added to a base word to make a new word.

cheer + ful = cheer**ful**

Circle the word that completes each phrase when *-ful* is added. Add *-ful* to the word and write the new word.

1. a ____ present   wonder   _____

                  hope   _____

2. a ____ quilt   care   _____

             color   _____

3. a ____ kitten   help   _____

             play   _____

4. a ____ insect   harm   _____

             hope   _____

5. the ____ dancer   grace   _____

             harm   _____

Notes for Home: Your child added the suffix *-ful* to base words. **Home Activity:** Challenge your child to add *-ful* and write phrases for words that were *not* circled on the page.

Name _____

The letters *a, al,* and *au* stand for the vowel sound in these words.

water   false   cause

Follow the directions. Use words from the list.

fall   pause   salt   small   fault

1. Write the word for the time after *summer.* Circle the letters that stand for the vowel sound.

   _____

2. Write the word that means the same as *mistake.* Circle the letters that stand for the vowel sound.

   _____

3. Write the word that means the opposite of *large.* Circle the letters that stand for the vowel sound.

   _____

4. Write the word that goes with *pepper.* Circle the letters that stand for the vowel sound.

   _____

5. Write the word that means "to stop for a time." Circle the letters that stand for the vowel sound.

   _____

© Scott Foresman 2

Notes for Home: Your child identified words with the vowel patterns *a, al,* and *au.*
Home Activity: Have your child make up a sentence for each word he or she wrote.

> The words *water*, *walk*, and *cause* have the same vowel sound.
>
> **wa**ter   **wa**lk   c**au**se

Circle the word that tells about the picture. Write the word.

1.   stalk   saucer

_____
- - - - - - - - - - -
_____

2.   false   laundry

_____
- - - - - - - - - - -
_____

3.   salt   small

_____
- - - - - - - - - - -
_____

4.   call   cause

_____
- - - - - - - - - - -
_____

5.   water   walk

_____
- - - - - - - - - - -
_____

6.   ball   fault

_____
- - - - - - - - - - -
_____

7.   false   talk

_____
- - - - - - - - - - -
_____

8.   faucet   laundry

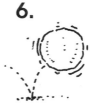

_____
- - - - - - - - - - -
_____

9.   tall   malt

_____
- - - - - - - - - - -
_____

10.   hall   walnut

_____
- - - - - - - - - - -
_____

Notes for Home: Your child identified words with the vowel patterns *a, al,* and *au.*
Home Activity: Help your child make up meaning clues for the circled words on the page.

Some words have letters that are silent.
When you say *know,* you do not hear the *k.*
When you say *climb,* you do not hear the *b.*

Circle the letter that you do not hear.

1.  thumb

2.  knit

3.  lamb

4.  knife

5.  comb

6.  knee

7.  climb

8.  knuckles

9.  crumbs

10.  knot

Notes for Home: Your child identified words with silent letters. **Home Activity:** Have your child make up riddles using three words from the page.

The letters _ea_ stand for the vowel sound in the words _wealth_ and _head_.

Follow each direction. Write the word.

1. Write _feather_. Circle the letters that spell the short _e_ sound.
   _____

2. Change the _f_ to _l_ and write the new word.
   _____

3. Change the _l_ to _w_ and write the new word.
   _____

4. Write _thread_. Circle the letters that spell the short _e_ sound.
   _____

5. Change _th_ to _sp_ and write the new word.
   _____

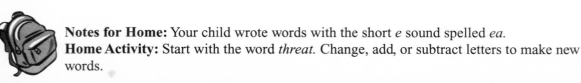

Notes for Home: Your child wrote words with the short _e_ sound spelled _ea_.
Home Activity: Start with the word _threat_. Change, add, or subtract letters to make new words.

The vowel sound in *law* and *thought* is spelled *aw* and *ough*.

Read the word at the beginning of each row. Circle the word that has the same vowel sound.

cough	1.	brought	couch	coach
crawl	2.	spare	few	hawk
straw	3.	fawn	dart	chair
lawn	4.	lane	sought	careful
fought	5.	fowl	soup	bought
draw	6.	star	dawn	mare
thaw	7.	ought	rare	want
dawn	8.	down	jaw	far
bought	9.	should	group	yawn
ought	10.	raw	tough	door

Notes for Home: Your child identified words with the vowel patterns *aw* and *ough*.
Home Activity: Challenge your child to tell a story using the words *crawl, hawk, fawn, saw, straw, lawn,* and *thaw.*

Sometimes two letters together stand for only one sound.

The *gn* in *sign* stands for the *n* sound.
The *wh* in *who* stands for the *h* sound.
The *wr* in *wring* stands for the *r* sound.

Circle the letters that complete the word. Then write the word.

1. a strong __ __ estler

    gn   wr   wh

_____

2. a bold desi __ __

    gn   wr   wh

_____

3. a __ __ ole pizza

    gn   wr   wh

_____

4. a __ __ at bite

    gn   wr   wh

_____

5. the boy's __ __ ist

    gn   wr   wh

_____

Notes for Home: Your child identified words with silent letters. **Home Activity:** Have your child choose three of the phrases above and rewrite them as sentences.

Name _____

The short *u* sound can be spelled *ou* as in *young*.

Write the word that tells about the picture. Circle the letters that spell the short *u* sound.

1.

country _____

young _____

2.

enough _____

couple _____

3.

touch _____

double _____

4.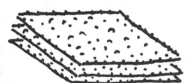

cousin _____

rough _____

5.

double _____

southern _____

Notes for Home: Your child wrote words with the short *u* sound spelled *ou*.
Home Activity: Have your child write sentences using five words from this page.

© Scott Foresman 2

In words like *rough* and *cousin,* the letters *ou* stand for the short *u* vowel sound.

Choose a word from the list to complete each sentence. Write the word and circle the letters that stand for the short *u* sound.

southern   enough   touch   country   young

_____

_____

1. We saw cows and sheep in the ____.

_____

_____

2. Georgia is a ____ state.

_____

_____

3. Don't ____ the hot stove!

_____

_____

4. There aren't ____ seats for everyone.

_____

_____

5. My brother is too ____ to go to school.

Notes for Home: Your child wrote words with the short *u* sound spelled *ou*.
Home Activity: Have your child give tell what each short *u* word means.

Name _____

The number of vowel sounds you hear in a word tells how many syllables are in the word.

sheep
1 syllable

chicken
2 syllables

kangaroo
3 syllables

Say each picture name. Write 1, 2, or 3 on the line to show how many syllables the word has.

1.  _____

2. _____

3. _____

4.  _____

5. _____

6.  _____

7.  _____

8.  _____

9.  _____

10.  _____

Notes for Home: Your child identified the number of syllables in words.
Home Activity: Have your child say each word on this page aloud and clap to show the number of syllables in the word.

The letters *aw* and *ough* stand for the vowel sound in these words.

th**aw**   **ough**t

Write the word that answers the question. Then circle the letters that stand for the vowel sound in the word.

1. Is a hawk or a fawn a baby deer?

2. Do you sip through a straw or thaw?

3. Do you draw or yawn when you are sleepy?

4. Do you cough or brought when you are sick?

5. Was the war bought or fought?

Notes for Home: Your child wrote words with the vowel patterns *aw* and *ough*.
Home Activity: Have your child identify the rhyming words on this page.

Name _____

In words like *design*, *whom*, and *wrap*, some letters are silent.

Write the word from the box that completes each sentence. Then underline the letter that is silent.

sign	wrong	wrote	who	gnaw

1. Rima _____ a letter to her cousin.

2. Did you see _____ won the race?

3. The _____ said "Two for One Sale!"

4. Dogs like to _____ on bones.

5. Something is _____ with the computer.

Notes for Home: Your child wrote words with silent letters. **Home Activity:** Have your child write a tongue twister using words with silent letters.

Name _____

The schwa sound can be spelled *a*.

across   **a**bout

The schwa sound can be spelled consonant + *le*.

peo**ple**   hum**ble**

Write the word with the schwa sound to complete
each sentence.

1. Yuka lives in the apartment _____ me.

below   above

___

2. Erica wore a _____ sweater.

green   purple

___

3. Lions live in a _____.

jungle   zoo

___

4. Jorge ran _____ the track.

around   on

___

5. The _____ soared in the sky.

hawk   eagle

Notes for Home: Your child wrote words with the schwa sound spelled *a* and consonant + *le*.
Home Activity: Help your child think of other words with the schwa sound spelled *a* and
consonant + *le*.

© Scott Foresman 2

Name _____

The schwa sound in *across* is spelled *a*.
The schwa sound in *people* is spelled consonant + *le*.

Circle the word in each sentence that has the schwa sound
spelled *a* or consonant + *le*. Write the word.

_____

1. Put your toys away before bedtime.

_____

2. The kettle was on the stove.

_____

3. Pat likes to tell riddles.

_____

4. It is about nine o'clock.

_____

5. The stars seemed to twinkle.

Notes for Home: Your child wrote words with the schwa sound spelled *a* and consonant + *le*.
Home Activity: Have your child underline the letter or letters that stand for the schwa sound
in each word he or she wrote.

Name _____

Add -s or -es to a word to show more than one.

Add -s to words like *house*.   house—hous**es**

Add -es to words that end in s, ss, *ch*, *sh*, or *x*.

    ax—ax**es**   church—church**es**
    bush—bush**es**   glass—glass**es**

Write the plural form of the picture name in the sentence.

1. We washed many _____ .

2. The park has three _____ .

3. Two _____ slept in the den.

4. The _____ are beautiful.

5. Several _____ waited in line.

Notes for Home: Your child added -s and -es to make the plural forms of words.
Home Activity: Label two columns -s and -es. Take turns with your child writing a word and
its plural form in each column.

Name _____

The letters *ou* stand for the short *u* vowel sound in words like *tough*.

The words below have the short *u* sound spelled *ou*. Find and circle each word in the puzzle.

cousin	enough	southern	couple	trouble
touch	rough	country	young	double

```
e  w  c  o  u  n  t  r  y  r
n  e  o  c  o  u  p  l  e  g
o  s  y  o  e  t  s  w  y  o
u  t  h  u  t  r  a  t  k  t
g  h  a  s  d  o  u  b  l  e
h  r  s  i  y  u  r  u  m  h
q  o  d  n  h  b  f  b  w  n
a  u  f  w  n  l  t  h  a  m
c  g  r  a  j  e  y  e  e  u
t  h  i  d  o  t  o  u  c  h
o  b  s  o  u  t  h  e  r  n
y  o  u  n  g  r  g  r  e  s
```

© Scott Foresman 2

Notes for Home: Your child identified words with the short *u* sound spelled *ou*.
Home Activity: Have your child choose five words and write a sentence for each one.

Name _____

Some words have one syllable: *cot, nurse.*
Some words have two syllables: *summer, dentist.*
Some words have three syllables: *umbrella, kangaroo.*

Write 1, 2, or 3 on the line to show how many syllables each word has. Then write the word with two syllables.

1. difficult   dime   dinner   _____

    _____   _____   _____

2. bottom   boot   bodyguard   _____

    _____   _____   _____

3. horn   hornet   horrible   _____

    _____   _____   _____

4. kimono   kitten   kite   _____

    _____   _____   _____

5. chain   character   camel   _____

    _____   _____   _____

Notes for Home: Your child identified words with one, two, or three syllables.
Home Activity: Have your child look through a magazine and cut out pictures whose names have one, two, or three syllables and sort them according to number of syllables.

The letters *ue* stand for the vowel sound in *blue*.

Choose the word from the box that makes sense in the sentence and has the vowel sound in *blue*. Write the word.

tissue	paste	guard	true	clues
hints	statue	handkerchief	glue	real

1. Bring scissors and _____ to class.

   _____

2. Use the _____ to figure out the word's meaning.

   _____

3. A _____ stood outside of the building.

   _____

4. She wiped her nose with a _____.

   _____

5. The movie was based on a _____ story.

   _____

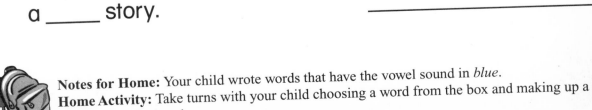
Notes for Home: Your child wrote words that have the vowel sound in *blue*.
Home Activity: Take turns with your child choosing a word from the box and making up a sentence for the word.

Name _____

| The letters *ue* spell the vowel sound in *blue*. |

Follow the directions.

1. Write *blue*. Underline the letters that spell the vowel sound.

   _____

2. Change *b* to *g*. Write the new word. Underline the letters that spell the vowel sound.

   _____

3. Change *g* to *c*. Write the new word. Underline the letters that spell the vowel sound.

   _____

4. Change *cl* to *tr*. Write the new word. Underline the letters that spell the vowel sound.

   _____

5. Change *tr* to *s*. Write the new word. Underline the letters that spell the vowel sound.

   _____

Notes for Home: Your child wrote words that have the vowel sound in *blue*.
Home Activity: Have your child write a poem using two words from this page.

Name _____

The schwa sound can be spelled consonant + *er*.

wea**ther**   fe**ver**

Underline the words that have the schwa sound spelled consonant + *er*. Then follow the directions.

across	hammer	seven	barrel	ladder
dinner	ahead	finger	cabin	water
kitchen	better	feather	beaver	jewel
diet	sweater	muffin	carrot	number

1. Write the word that names an animal that builds dams.   ------------------------

2. Write the word that names 1, 5, 8, 12, 37, or 124.   ------------------------

3. Write the word that names a tool for hitting.   ------------------------

4. Write the word that names a part of the hand.   ------------------------

5. Write the word that names a piece of clothing.   ------------------------

Notes for Home: Your child identified words that have the schwa sound spelled consonant + *er*. **Home Activity:** Together make a list of things around the house whose names have the schwa sound spelled consonant + *er*.

Name _____

The schwa sound can be spelled *a* or consonant + *le*.

along   bri**dle**

Unscramble the letters to make a word that has the schwa sound spelled *a* or consonant + *le* and that matches the clue. Write the word.

1. not big   lleitt   _____

2. from one side to the other   scasor   _____

3. use it with thread   deenel   _____

4. in front   aadhe   _____

5. a color   lerpup   _____

Notes for Home: Your child wrote words with the schwa sound spelled *a* or consonant + *le*.
Home Activity: Have your child tell a story using the words *poodle, table, noodle, about,* and *alone*.

114

© Scott Foresman 2

Name _____

Add *-s* or *-es* to a word to show more than one.

nurse—nurse**s**   inch—inch**es**

fox—fox**es**   bush—bush**es**   bus—bus**es**

Circle *s* or *es* to show how to make each picture name mean more than one.

1.  s   es

horse

2.  s   es

brush

3.  s   es

match

4.  s   es

rose

5.  s   es

peach

6.  s   es

purse

7.  s   es

box

8.  s   es

house

9.  s   es

dish

10.  s   es

glass

Notes for Home: Your child identified *-s* and *-es* as the plural endings on words.
Home Activity: Have your child look through a magazine or newspaper, circle plural words, and list the words according to their *-s* and *-es* endings.

The long *a* sound can be spelled *ei* as in *reindeer* or *eigh* as in *eight*.

Circle the word that has the same vowel sound as the picture name. Underline the letters that spell the vowel sound in the word.

1. freight

   cap

2. wrap

   weight

3. veil

   vine

4. reign

   pat

5. sleigh

   try

6. cannon

   neighbor

7. vein

   march

8. grand

   eighty

9. beige

   stamp

10. reindeer

    ham

Notes for Home: Your child identified words with the long *a* sound spelled *ei* and *eigh*.
Home Activity: Have your child choose four words from this page and make up a riddle for each one.

Name _____

In the word *vein*, the letters *ei* spell the long *a* vowel sound. In the word *eight*, the letters *eigh* spell the long *a* vowel sound.

Write the words to complete the puzzle.

reindeer   veil   beige   neighbor   eight

Across
2. seven plus one
3. person next door
4. light tan

Down
1. animal with antlers
5. worn over the face

Notes for Home: Your child identified words with the long *a* sound spelled *ei* and *eigh*. **Home Activity:** Have your child tell a story using the words *reindeer, eight, sleigh,* and *neighbor.*

117

Adding an ending or a suffix to a base word adds another syllable to the word.

high	one syllable	high + er = higher	two syllables
help	one syllable	help + less = helpless	two syllables

Draw a line to divide each word between the base word and the ending or suffix. Then write the word that matches each clue.

chooses   talking   smaller   sunless   darkest

restless   quickly   closes   pushes   helpful

I. shuts _____

2. without sun _____

3. more than small _____

4. without rest _____

5. shoves _____

6. speaking _____

7. most dark _____

8. full of help _____

9. picks _____

10. with speed _____

Notes for Home: Your child identified words of more than one syllable that have suffixes and endings. **Home Activity:** Have your child look in a favorite book, find words that have the same endings or suffixes as the words on this page, and tell how many syllables each word has.

Name _____

The vowel sound in *blue* is spelled *ue*.

Circle the word that has the same vowel sound as the picture name. Then write the word and circle the letters that spell the vowel sound you hear in *blue*.

1.

   statue

   standing

   _____
   -
   _____

2.

   cut

   clue

   _____
   -
   _____

3.

   true

   truck

   _____
   -
   _____

4.

   taste

   tissue

   _____
   -
   _____

5.

   glue

   glum

   _____
   -
   _____

Notes for Home: Your child identified words that have the vowel sound in *blue*.
Home Activity: Have your child write a phrase using each circled word.

© Scott Foresman 2

119

Name _____

The schwa sound can be spelled consonant + *er*.

wat*er*   **feat*her***

Write the word that answers each clue. Then underline the letters that spell the schwa sound.

member   banner   chatter   order   tiger

1. talk quickly   _____

2. a flag   _____

3. a person belonging to a group   _____

4. tell what to do   _____

5. a large cat with stripes   _____

Notes for Home: Your child identified words that have the schwa sound spelled consonant + *er*. **Home Activity:** Have your child make a banner using words with the schwa sound spelled consonant + *er*.

Name _____

The letters *ex* spell the beginning sounds in these words.

explore   **ex**cite

Write a word from the box in place of the underlined word or words.

exit	next	explain	Texas	exact

1. Austin is the capital of <u>a large state.</u>

_____

2. The sign showed him <u>the way out.</u>

_____

3. My watch tells <u>correct</u> time.

_____

4. Her birthday is <u>the following</u> week.

_____

5. Can you <u>tell</u> how the machine works?

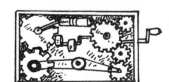

_____

Notes for Home: Your child wrote words with the *ex* pattern. **Home Activity:** Together with your child look through a magazine or newspaper for other words with the *ex* pattern. Make a list of the words you find.

Name _____

Pattern *ex*

In words like *exercise* and *expert,* the letters *ex* stand for the beginning sounds.

Add *ex* to the letters to finish the word. Write the word.

1. the ind___ ___ of the book

_____

_____

2. the state of T___ ___as

_____

3. n___ ___t in line

_____

_____

4. ___ ___it from the room

_____

_____

5. an ___ ___act copy

_____

_____

6. an ___ ___tra pair of socks

_____

_____

7. a good ___ ___ample

_____

_____

8. an ___ ___pert in math

_____

_____

9. everyone ___ ___cept me

_____

_____

10. ___ ___plore the cave

_____

_____

Notes for Home: Your child completed words with the *ex* pattern. **Home Activity:** Challenge your child to tell a story using the words *explain, excellent, extra, example,* and *experiment.*

122

© Scott Foresman 2

Name _____

A prefix is a word part added to the beginning of a word. Adding a prefix like *un-*, *dis-*, or *re-* changes the meaning of the word.

un + happy = **un**happy   not happy, the opposite of *happy*

dis + loyal = **dis**loyal   not loyal, the opposite of *loyal*

re + wind = **re**wind   to wind again

Add the prefix to the underlined word. Write the new word.

1. **(dis)** to not <u>like</u>   _____

2. **(dis)** the opposite of <u>obey</u>   _____

3. **(re)** to <u>fill</u> again   _____

4. **(un)** the opposite of <u>safe</u>   _____

5. **(un)** not <u>lucky</u>   _____

Notes for Home: Your child wrote words with the prefixes *un-*, *dis-*, and *re-*.
Home Activity: Have your child choose a word from the page and draw a picture to show how the meaning changed when the prefix *un-*, *dis-*, or *re-* was added.

The letters *ei* and *eigh* spell the long *a* sound in *rein* and *sleigh*.

Unscramble the letters to make a word from the list that has the long *a* sound spelled *ei* or *eigh*. Write the word.

eight   freight   veil   beige   weight

_____
- -
1. The bride wore a lace *leiv*.   _____

_____
- -
2. He washed his *geeib* shirt.   _____

_____
- -
3. The bowl held *tigeh* eggs.   _____

_____
- -
4. The *rifthge* train hauled coal.   _____

_____
- -
5. What is the *gwieth* of that box?   _____

Notes for Home: Your child identified words with the long *a* sound spelled *ei* and *eigh*.
Home Activity: Have your child rewrite each sentence on this page as a question and underline the long *a* words.

Adding an ending or a suffix to a base word usually adds another syllable to the word.

match	one syllable
match + es = matches	two syllables
cold	one syllable
cold + er = colder	two syllables

Follow the signs to make a new word. Write the word. Then in the box write the number of syllables you hear.

1. finish + es

2. run + ing

3. swift + ly

4. beauty + ful

5. hopped − ed + ing

Notes for Home: Your child identified words of more than one syllable that have suffixes and endings. **Home Activity:** Have your child add an ending or suffix to *forget, wish,* and *sudden* and tell how many syllables each new word has.

Name _____

The long *e* vowel sound in *niece* is spelled *ie*.
The long *e* vowel sound in *valley* is spelled *ey*.

Draw a line to match each picture with its name. Circle the letters that stand for the long *e* sound in each word.

1.    field

2.    donkey

3.    cookie

4. 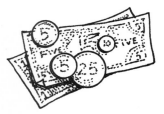   money

5.   monkey

 Notes for Home: Your child identified words that have the long *e* vowel sound spelled *ie* and *ey*. **Home Activity:** Have your child choose two words from this page and make up a riddle for each one.

Name _____

In the word *grief,* the letters *ie* spell the long *e* vowel sound.
In the word *trolley,* the letters *ey* spell the long *e*
vowel sound.

Underline the words that have the long *e* sound spelled *ie* or *ey*.
Then follow the directions.

alley	shy	chief	field	team
brief	pulley	niece	they	piece
money	obey	beige	key	hockey

I. Write the word that rhymes with *shield*. _____

2. Write the word that names a relative. _____

3. Write the word that names something
that opens a lock. _____

4. Write the word that names a game
played on ice. _____

5. Write the word that means a part
of something. _____

Notes for Home: Your child identified words that have the long *e* vowel sound spelled *ie* and
ey. **Home Activity:** Challenge your child to think of clues for the five underlined words that
were not written on the page.

The *f* sound can be spelled *gh*, *ph*, and *lf*.

cou**gh**   go**ph**er   ha**lf**way

Write the word that answers the question. Circle the letters that stand for the *f* sound.

1. Does sandpaper feel rough or enough?

2. Have you had enough or tough when you are full?

3. Does a dolphin or an elephant live in the ocean?

4. Do you use a phone or a graph to call a friend?

5. Is a calf or a nephew a baby cow?

Notes for Home: Your child identified words that have the *f* sound spelled *gh*, *ph*, and *lf*.
Home Activity: Have your child write sentences using the words *tough, alphabet,* and *golf*.

Name _____

The letters *ex* can be at the beginning, in the middle, or at the end of words.

Find and circle the *ex* words in the puzzle. Then write the *ex* word that goes with each meaning clue.

examine		
extra		
index		
explode		
next		

b	t	r	o	l	m	e
e	a	x	i	e	d	x
x	i	k	e	x	y	p
s	n	e	x	t	j	l
y	d	q	d	r	u	o
t	e	g	h	a	x	d
e	x	a	m	i	n	e

1. following

_____
- - - - - - - - - - - - - - - -
_____

2. part of a book

_____
- - - - - - - - - - - - - - - -
_____

3. look at carefully

_____
- - - - - - - - - - - - - - - -
_____

4. to burst

_____
- - - - - - - - - - - - - - - -
_____

5. more than enough

_____
- - - - - - - - - - - - - - - -
_____

Notes for Home: Your child wrote words with the *ex* pattern. **Home Activity:** Have your child write a question using each of the *ex* words on this page.

129

Name _____

The prefixes *un-* and *dis-* mean *not* or *opposite of*.
The prefix *re-* means *to do again*.

the opposite of *like*	**un**like
not respectful	**dis**respectful
to play again	**re**play

Add the prefix to the base word to form a new word. Use the
new words to complete the sentences.

(un) wrap   **(dis)** honest   **(re)** load
          (un) ripe   **(re)** heat

1. The _____ person stole the money.

2. Can you _____ the soup?

3. Is that green banana _____ ?

4. Jeff wants to _____ his present.

5. The driver will _____ the truck.

Notes for Home: Your child wrote words with the prefixes *un-*, *dis-*, and *re-*.
Home Activity: Have your child add *un-*, *dis-*, or *re-* to these words: *kind, agree, build.*

In the word *receipt*, the letters *ei* spell the long *e* vowel sound.

Add *ei* to the letters to finish the word. Write the word.

1. Flying kites is Mike's l__ __sure activity.

_____

2. You get prot__ __n from meat.

_____

3. She painted the c__ __ling.

_____

4. Did you rec__ __ve a gift?

_____

5. The player s__ __zed the ball.

_____

Notes for Home: Your child wrote words with the long *e* sound spelled *ei*.
Home Activity: Take turns with your child choosing a word from the page and using it in a sentence.

Name _____

The long *e* vowel sound can be spelled *ei* as in *protein*.

Follow the directions. Use the words from the box. Then circle the letters that stand for the long *e* sound.

ceiling	seize	receipt	leisure	receive

1. Write the word that names time you spend not working.

   _____

2. Write the word that means "get."

   _____

3. Write the word that names part of a room.

   _____

4. Write the word that means "grab."

   _____

5. Write the word that names the paper you get when you buy something.

   _____

Notes for Home: Your child identified words with the long *e* sound spelled *ei*.
Home Activity: Scramble the letters of each word in the box and have your child unscramble and write the words.

For some words that end in *f* or *fe*, the *f* or *fe* is changed to *v*, and -*es* is added to show more than one.

half—hal**ves**

Write the word that names the picture. Then add -*es* to make the word mean more than one. Write the new word.

1. I raked the  into a big pile.

2. She put two  on the table.

3. Seth baked three .

4. The  were ready.

5. The  are not sleeping.

 Notes for Home: Your child added -*es* to make the plural forms of words ending in *f* or *fe*.
Home Activity: Have your child form the plurals of *elf*, *calf*, and *scarf* and write a sentence using each word.

Name _____

The long *e* sound can be spelled *ie* and *ey*.

ni**e**ce   mon**ey**

Write the word that completes each sentence and has the long *e* sound spelled *ie* or *ey*.

1. My dad is a police _____ .

    _____

    chief   officer

2. The bees made _____ .

    _____

    noise   honey

3. The farmer planted a _____ of corn.

    _____

    field   row

4. Smoke came out of the _____ .

    _____

    chimney   roof

5. His speech was _____ .

    _____

    long   brief

Notes for Home: Your child identified words that have the long *e* vowel sound spelled *ie* and *ey*. **Home Activity:** Write the headings *ie* and *ey* on paper and help your child think of words to write under each heading.

Name _____

The *f* sound can be spelled *gh*, *ph*, and *lf*.

rou**gh**   gra**ph**   go**lf**

Use the words in the box to complete the puzzle.

half   laugh   enough   gopher   autograph

Across
4. signing your name
5. one of two parts

Down
1. an animal that lives in the ground
2. just the right amount
3. what a joke makes you do

Notes for Home: Your child identified words that have the *f* sound spelled *gh*, *ph*, or *lf*.
Home Activity: Help your child make a list of other words that have the *f* sound spelled *gh*, *ph*, or *lf*.

The letters *air* and *are* stand for the vowel sound in these words.

fa**ir**   **sp**a**re**

Write the word that names each picture. Circle the letters that stand for the vowel sound.

pair   chair   hair   mare   square

1.
_____   air   are

2.
_____   air   are

3.
_____   air   are

4.
_____   air   are

5.
_____   air   are

Notes for Home: Your child identified words with the *air* and *are* vowel patterns.
Home Activity: Have your child write a poem using rhyming *air* and *are* words.

Name _____

In words like *hair* and *dare*, the letters *air* and *are* stand for the vowel sound.

Write the word that matches the meaning and has the vowel sound in *hair*. Circle the letters that spell the vowel sound.

	gaze	_____
1. to look at something	stare	_____

	chair	_____
2. something to sit on	couch	_____

	repair	_____
3. to fix something	mend	_____

	shout	_____
4. to make a loud sound	blare	_____

	pair	_____
5. two that go together	couple	_____

Notes for Home: Your child identified words with the *air* and *are* vowel patterns.
Home Activity: Have your child make a list of words that rhyme with *care*.

The letters *dge* spell the *j* sound in *hedge*.

Write the word from the box that completes each sentence.
Underline the letters that spell the ending *j* sound.

| bridge | judge | fudge | ledge | badge |

1. The police officer wore a shiny _____ .

2. A new _____ was built over the river.

3. Sara put nuts in the _____ .

4. I set the plant on the window _____ .

5. The _____ spoke to the jury.

Notes for Home: Your child wrote words in which /j/ is spelled *dge*. **Home Activity:** Have your child write a tongue twister using the words *badge*, *budge*, and *bridge*.

Name _____

The letters *ei* spell the long *e* sound in *receipt*.

Find five words in the puzzle with the long *e* sound spelled *ei*.
Circle each word in the puzzle. Then write the word.

r	i	e	h	t	r	e
e	r	o	n	y	t	u
c	e	i	l	i	n	g
e	c	w	e	r	o	k
i	e	w	i	r	a	c
v	i	l	s	k	e	k
e	p	f	u	a	m	t
i	t	h	r	r	u	u
d	e	c	e	i	v	e

1. _____

2. _____

3. _____

4. _____

5. _____

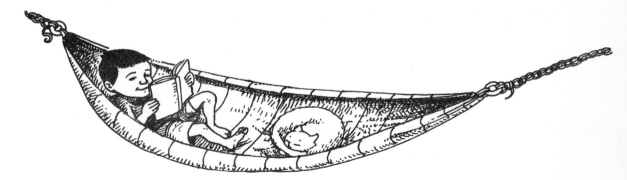

Notes for Home: Your child identified words that have the long *e* vowel sound spelled *ei*.
Home Activity: Give a clue for each of the circled words and have your child name the *ei*
word that goes with the clue.

Name _____

> To form the plural of some words ending in *f* or *fe*, *f* or *fe* is changed to *v*, and *-es* is added.
>
> ## wif**e**—wi**ves**

Write the plural form of the underlined word.

1. The <u>loaf</u> of bread was freshly baked.

_____
_____

2. The <u>wolf</u> howled at the moon.

_____
_____

3. The dictionary is on that <u>shelf</u>.

_____
_____

Write the singular form of the underlined word.

4. Did the tree's <u>leaves</u> turn red?

_____
_____

5. Carl put the <u>knives</u> next to the spoons.

_____
_____

Notes for Home: Your child wrote the plural and singular forms of words ending in *f* and *fe*. **Home Activity:** Encourage your child to write a short story using as many plural words as possible from this page.

Name _____

A vowel at the end of a syllable in a word stands for a long vowel sound.

a/ble	di/et	bo/nus
long *a*	long *i*	long *o*

Circle the long vowel sound you hear at the end of a syllable in each word.

1. real

long *a*   long *e*   long *u*

2. dial

long *a*   long *e*   long *i*

3. cradle

long *a*   long *e*   long *o*

4. poet

long *a*   long *e*   long *o*

5. uniform

long *i*   long *o*   long *u*

6. cereal

long *a*   long *e*   long *o*

7. bacon

long *a*   long *o*   long *u*

8. program

long *a*   long *e*   long *o*

9. title

long *e*   long *i*   long *o*

10. music

long *a*   long *i*   long *u*

Notes for Home: Your child identified long vowel sounds at the ends of syllables in words.
Home Activity: Ask your child to name the long vowel sound in each of these words: *paper, broken, tiger, unit.*

Name _____

Vowels at the ends of syllables stand for long vowel sounds.

ba / con   e / ven   pi / lot
long *a*   long *e*   long *i*

Write the name of each picture. Circle the letter that stands for a long vowel sound.

paper   uniform   table   music   pliers
lion   cereal   zero   banjo   cradle

1. _____

2. _____

3. _____

4. _____

5. _____

6. _____

7. _____

8. _____

9. _____

10. _____

Notes for Home: Your child wrote words with long vowel sounds at the ends of syllables.
Home Activity: Together with your child write other words like those on the page. Check them in a dictionary.

© Scott Foresman 2

Name _____

The letters *ch* spell /k/ in *chord*.
The letters *sch* spell /sk/ in *schedule*.

Underline the words that have /k/ spelled *ch* as in *chord* or /sk/ spelled *sch* as in *schedule*. Then write the underlined words in the correct list.

chalk	risk	chemist
school	shadow	track
fresh	scheme	score
scream	color	stomach
chorus	sketch	bench

/k/ spelled *ch*

1. _____

2. _____

3. _____

/sk/ spelled *sch*

4. _____

5. _____

Notes for Home: Your child identified words in which /k/ is spelled *ch* and /sk/ is spelled *sch*.
Home Activity: Have your child use each word he or she wrote in a sentence.

Name _____

The letters *air* and *are* stand for the vowel sound in *stairs* and *hare*.

Write a word from the list to complete each sentence. Then circle the letters that stand for the vowel sound.

spare	rare	repair	share	pair

1. Will you ____ your fruit with me?

            _____

2. I bought a new ____ of shoes.

            _____

3. Can you ____ the broken radio?

            _____

4. He put the ____ tire on the car.

            _____

5. Tara collects ____ stamps.

            _____

Notes for Home: Your child wrote words with the *air* and *are* vowel patterns.
Home Activity: Have your child write a newspaper headline using words from this page.

Name _____

The letters *dge* stand for the *j* sound in *budge*.

Write the word that answers the clue and has the *j* sound spelled *dge*.

bridge	jury	badge	toffee	uniform
fence	fudge	current	judge	hedge

1. A garden may have this. _____

2. A court of law has this. _____

3. A police officer has this. _____

4. A candy shop has this. _____

5. A river may have this. _____

Notes for Home: Your child identified words in which the *j* sound is spelled *dge*.
Home Activity: Have your child write clues for these *dge* words: *ledge, ridge, budge*.

The letters *ear* stand for the vowel sound in *earn*.
The letters *our* stand for the vowel sound in *flour*.

Write the word from the box that belongs in each group and has
the vowel sound in *earn* or *flour.*

| Pluto | day | learn | hunt | hour |
| sour | search | hot | Earth | know |

1. study, practice, _____
   _____

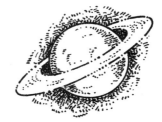

2. salty, sweet, _____
   _____

3. Mars, Venus, _____
   _____

4. minute, second, _____
   _____

5. seek, look for, _____
   _____

Notes for Home: Your child wrote words with the *ear* and *our* vowel patterns.
Home Activity: Have your child circle the letters that stand for the vowel sound in each word
he or she wrote on the page.

In *earn,* the letters *ear* stand for the vowel sound.
In *flour,* the letters *our* stand for the vowel sound.

Circle the words that have the same vowel sound and pattern
as *earn* or *flour*. Then write the circled words to complete
the sentences.

court	hour	pearl	round	term
near	heard	fort	learn	sour

1. We _____ a dog barking.

2. Omar came home an _____ late.

3. The ring has a _____ on it.

4. The baby will _____ to walk.

5. A lemon tastes very _____ .

Notes for Home: Your child wrote words with the *ear* and *our* vowel patterns.
Home Activity: Have your child make up two rhymes using the word pairs *earn/learn* and
sour/our.

The letters *tion* make a syllable in words.

| petition | dictionary | evaluation |
| pe/ti/**tion** | dic/**tion**/ar/y | e/val/u/a/**tion** |

Add the letters *tion* to make another syllable in each word. Write the whole word.

1. ac/_____

   _____
   - - - - - - - - - - - - - - - -
   _____

2. col/lec/_____

   _____
   - - - - - - - - - - - - - - - -
   _____

3. so/lu/_____

   _____
   - - - - - - - - - - - - - - - -
   _____

4. frac/_____

   _____
   - - - - - - - - - - - - - - - -
   _____

5. di/rec/_____

   _____
   - - - - - - - - - - - - - - - -
   _____

6. cau/_____

   _____
   - - - - - - - - - - - - - - - -
   _____

7. na/_____/al

   _____
   - - - - - - - - - - - - - - - -
   _____

8. pro/tec/_____

   _____
   - - - - - - - - - - - - - - - -
   _____

9. po/si/_____

   _____
   - - - - - - - - - - - - - - - -
   _____

10. e/mo/_____/al

   _____
   - - - - - - - - - - - - - - - -
   _____

Notes for Home: Your child wrote words that have *tion* as a syllable.
Home Activity: Take turns with your child naming *tion* words like those on the page.

Name _____

If a vowel is at the end of a syllable in a word, it can stand for a long vowel sound.

ve / to	long *e*	long *o*
tor / na / do	long *a*	long *o*

Write the word that completes each sentence. Circle each letter that stands for a long vowel sound. *Hint:* Each word has more than one long vowel sound.

stereo   idea   radio   piano   video

1. A local _____ station is having a talent contest.

2. I could win a _____ with speakers.

3. I could win a _____ camera.

4. But I have no _____ what I can do.

5. I know! I'll play a song on the _____ .

Notes for Home: Your child wrote words with long vowel sounds at the ends of syllables. **Home Activity:** Have your child write a sentence using at least two of the long vowel words on the page.

Name _____

The letters *ch* can spell /k/ as in *chemist*.
The letters *sch* can spell /sk/ as in *scheme*.

Write the words to complete the paragraph. Circle the letters
that spell /k/ as in *chemist* or /sk/ as in *scheme*.

chord   schedule   school   stomach   chorus

_____

I have a busy **(1.)** _____ on Tuesdays.

_____

From 8 until 3:30, I am at **(2.)** _____. Then I sing

_____

in a **(3.)** _____. This Tuesday I was so busy I

missed lunch. At practice, when Mrs. Nuñez played a

_____   _____

(4.) _____ on the piano, my **(5.)** _____

growled really loud—right on cue! Everyone laughed.

Notes for Home: Your child wrote words in which *ch* spelled /k/ or *sch* spelled /sk/.
Home Activity: Together with your child make up a funny story using the *ch* and *sch* words
on the page.